Chicken Picca

A Flavorful Journ
Classic and Creative Chicken
Piccata Dishes

CHICKEN PICCATA RECIPES

First edition. November 19, 2023.

Copyright © 2023 Sammy Andrews.

ISBN: 979-8223017530

Written by Sammy Andrews.

Table of Contents

Sammy Andrews

Chapter 1: Introduction to Chicken Piccata

Chicken Piccata is a classic Italian dish that has gained popularity worldwide for its delicious combination of flavors. This dish typically features tender chicken cutlets bathed in a tangy lemon-caper sauce, making it a delightful choice for both casual family dinners and elegant dinner parties. In this chapter, we'll dive into the origins of Chicken Piccata, explore why it's cherished by many, and discuss some basic cooking techniques to help you get started on your Chicken Piccata journey.

The History and Origins of Chicken Piccata

The roots of Chicken Piccata can be traced back to Italy, where piccata-style preparations have been enjoyed for centuries. The word "piccata" comes from the Italian verb "piccare," which means "to prick" or "to puncture." The name is thought to be inspired by the small punctures made in the meat during the cooking process.

Traditional Italian piccata dishes often use veal as the primary protein, but chicken has become a popular alternative, particularly in the United States. The first written recipe for Chicken Piccata appeared in Italian cookbooks during the 19th century, highlighting the dish's enduring appeal.

Why Chicken Piccata is a Beloved Dish

Chicken Piccata has garnered a dedicated following for several reasons:

1. Bright and Zesty Flavor

The combination of fresh lemon juice, briny capers, and aromatic garlic creates a lively and flavorful sauce that perfectly complements the tender chicken.

2. Quick and Easy Preparation

Chicken Piccata is known for its simplicity and speed of preparation, making it an ideal choice for busy weeknight dinners. With a few basic ingredients and a straightforward cooking process, you can have a delicious meal on the table in no time.

3. Versatility

While the classic recipe is beloved, Chicken Piccata is also incredibly versatile. It can be adapted to suit various dietary preferences and flavor profiles, as you'll discover in the chapters to come.

4. Elegant Presentation

The dish's vibrant colors and appealing aroma make it an excellent choice for special occasions. Whether you're hosting a dinner party or celebrating a milestone, Chicken Piccata is sure to impress your guests.

Basic Cooking Techniques for Chicken Piccata

Before we dive into the specific recipes, let's cover some fundamental techniques that will help you master Chicken Piccata:

1. Pound Chicken Cutlets

To ensure even cooking and tenderness, it's essential to pound the chicken cutlets to a uniform thickness. Place the chicken between two sheets of plastic wrap or parchment paper and gently pound with a meat mallet until they are about 1/4-inch thick.

2. Dredging in Flour

Coating the chicken in seasoned flour not only adds flavor but also creates a crispy exterior when pan-fried. Season the flour with salt, pepper, and optional spices to enhance the dish's taste.

3. Proper Pan-Frying

Use a large skillet or frying pan to cook the chicken cutlets. Heat a combination of butter and olive oil until it's hot but not smoking. Pan-fry the chicken for a few minutes on each side until it's golden brown and cooked through.

4. Creating the Lemon-Caper Sauce

The signature sauce for Chicken Piccata is made by deglazing the pan with white wine and then adding lemon juice, capers, and chicken broth. Allow the sauce to simmer and reduce until it thickens slightly.

5. Serving and Garnishing

Serve your Chicken Piccata hot, garnished with fresh parsley and lemon slices. It pairs wonderfully with pasta, rice, or a variety of side dishes.

Now that we've explored the background and basic techniques of Chicken Piccata, you're ready to embark on your culinary journey through the diverse world of Chicken Piccata recipes. In the following chapters, we'll explore classic preparations, creative variations, dietary adaptations, and even desserts inspired by this beloved dish. So, let's get started with Chapter 3, where we'll dive into the heart of Chicken Piccata with the classic recipe!

Chapter 2: Essential Ingredients and Kitchen Tools

Before we dive into the delightful world of Chicken Piccata recipes, it's essential to familiarize ourselves with the key ingredients and kitchen tools that will help us create this mouthwatering dish. In this chapter, we'll explore the importance of selecting the right chicken, the role of fresh lemons and capers, and the various flavorful components that make Chicken Piccata so special. Additionally, we'll discuss the essential kitchen tools and utensils you'll need to make the cooking process smooth and enjoyable.

Choosing the Best Chicken

The quality of the chicken you select plays a crucial role in the final taste and texture of your Chicken Piccata. Here are some tips for choosing the best chicken:

Chicken Cutlets: For Chicken Piccata, boneless and skinless chicken cutlets or chicken breasts are commonly used. These cuts are lean and cook quickly, making them ideal for this dish. Look for fresh, well-trimmed cutlets at your local butcher or grocery store.

Free-Range or Organic Chicken: Whenever possible, opt for free-range or organic chicken. These chickens are typically raised in more humane conditions and may have a more robust flavor.

Thickness Matters: If your chicken cutlets are thicker than 1/4-inch, consider using a meat mallet to gently pound them to a uniform thickness. This ensures even cooking.

The Importance of Fresh Lemons

Lemons are a star ingredient in Chicken Piccata, providing the dish with its signature tangy and citrusy flavor. Here's what you need to know about using fresh lemons:

Juicing Lemons: To extract the maximum juice from lemons, roll them on your countertop before cutting and juicing. This softens the fruit and makes it easier to extract the juice.

Zesting Lemons: Lemon zest, the outer peel, is packed with aromatic oils that add depth to the sauce. Use a microplane or fine grater to zest the lemon, but be cautious not to include the bitter white pith.

Capers: A Key Ingredient

Capers are small, green flower buds commonly used in Mediterranean cuisine. They bring a burst of briny, slightly tangy flavor to Chicken Piccata. Here's what you should know about capers:

Types of Capers: Capers are available in various sizes, with smaller capers being more delicate in flavor. Choose the size that suits your taste.

Rinsing Capers: Capers are often packed in brine or salt. Before using them, rinse them under cold water to remove excess salt or brine.

Other Flavorful Components

While lemons and capers are the stars of Chicken Piccata, there are other flavorful components that you can incorporate to enhance the dish:

Garlic: Fresh minced garlic adds a delightful aromatic quality to the sauce. Adjust the amount to your preference.

White Wine: White wine is used to deglaze the pan and create the base for the lemon-caper sauce. Dry white wines like Sauvignon Blanc or Chardonnay work well.

Chicken Broth: Chicken broth or chicken stock provides depth and richness to the sauce. Use a low-sodium variety to control the saltiness of the dish.

Butter and Olive Oil: A combination of butter and olive oil is used for pan-frying the chicken cutlets. Butter adds richness, while olive oil prevents the butter from burning.

Essential Kitchen Tools and Utensils

To make your Chicken Piccata cooking experience enjoyable and efficient, it's essential to have the right tools and utensils on hand:

Meat Mallet: Use a meat mallet to pound chicken cutlets to a uniform thickness.

Cutting Board: A sturdy cutting board provides a safe surface for chopping, slicing, and mincing ingredients like garlic and lemons.

Citrus Juicer: A citrus juicer or reamer makes it easy to extract fresh lemon juice.

Microplane or Zester: A microplane or fine grater is ideal for zesting lemons.

Skillet or Frying Pan: A large skillet or frying pan is essential for pan-frying the chicken and preparing the sauce.

Tongs: Tongs are handy for flipping and transferring chicken cutlets.

Whisk: Use a whisk to combine the sauce ingredients evenly.

Knife and Kitchen Shears: Sharp knives and kitchen shears are essential for cutting and trimming chicken.

Now that we've covered the essential ingredients and kitchen tools for Chicken Piccata, you're well-equipped to start your culinary adventure.

Chapter 3: Classic Chicken Piccata

In this chapter, we'll delve into the heart of Chicken Piccata with the classic recipe that has captured the hearts and taste buds of countless food lovers. You'll discover step-by-step instructions for creating this timeless dish, along with valuable tips to achieve perfectly crispy chicken cutlets. We'll also explore how to present and garnish your Classic Chicken Piccata for a stunning and appetizing plate.

Traditional Chicken Piccata Recipe
Ingredients:

- 4 boneless, skinless chicken cutlets
- Salt and freshly ground black pepper, to taste
- 1/2 cup all-purpose flour, for dredging
- 2 tablespoons olive oil
- 2 tablespoons unsalted butter
- 1/4 cup fresh lemon juice (about 2 lemons)
- 1/2 cup dry white wine
- 1/4 cup capers, drained and rinsed
- 1/4 cup chicken broth
- 2 cloves garlic, minced
- 2 tablespoons fresh parsley, chopped (for garnish)
- Lemon slices, for garnish

Step-by-Step Instructions:
Prepare the Chicken Cutlets:

1. Place each chicken cutlet between two sheets of plastic wrap or parchment paper.
2. Use a meat mallet to gently pound the cutlets to an even thickness of about 1/4 inch.
3. Season both sides of the chicken cutlets with salt and freshly

ground black pepper.

Dredge in Flour:

1. Place the all-purpose flour in a shallow dish.
2. Dredge each chicken cutlet in the flour, shaking off any excess.

Pan-Fry the Chicken:

1. In a large skillet or frying pan, heat the olive oil and butter over medium-high heat.
2. Once the butter is foamy, add the chicken cutlets to the pan.
3. Cook for about 3-4 minutes on each side or until they are golden brown and cooked through.
4. Transfer the cooked chicken to a plate and cover with foil to keep warm.

Prepare the Lemon-Caper Sauce:

1. In the same skillet, add minced garlic and sauté for about 30 seconds until fragrant.
2. Deglaze the pan with the dry white wine, scraping up any browned bits from the bottom.
3. Add the fresh lemon juice, capers, and chicken broth. Allow the sauce to simmer for about 5 minutes or until it has reduced slightly.

Combine Chicken and Sauce:

1. Return the cooked chicken cutlets to the skillet, turning them in the sauce to coat evenly.
2. Simmer for an additional 2-3 minutes, allowing the chicken to absorb the flavors of the sauce.

Serve and Garnish:

1. Transfer the Chicken Piccata to serving plates.
2. Garnish with chopped fresh parsley and lemon slices for a burst of color and freshness.

Tips for Achieving Perfectly Crispy Chicken

Achieving perfectly crispy chicken cutlets is essential for a great Chicken Piccata. Here are some tips:

1. Even Thickness: Pound the chicken cutlets to an even thickness of about 1/4 inch to ensure even cooking.
2. Proper Dredging: Coat the chicken in flour, shaking off excess, for a crispy exterior when pan-frying.
3. Hot Pan: Make sure the skillet is hot when you add the chicken. This helps create a golden crust.
4. Avoid Overcrowding: Don't overcrowd the pan; cook the chicken in batches if necessary to maintain crispiness.

Classic Presentation and Garnishes

Aesthetics are an important part of any culinary experience. Here's how to present and garnish your Classic Chicken Piccata for an appealing plate:

- Plate Placement: Place the chicken cutlets in the center of the plate, slightly overlapping.

- Lemon Slices: Arrange lemon slices around the chicken for a pop of color and to emphasize the lemony flavor.

- Capers and Parsley: Sprinkle capers evenly over the chicken for bursts of briny goodness. A generous sprinkle of chopped fresh parsley adds a vibrant touch.

Now that you've mastered the Classic Chicken Piccata recipe, you have a timeless dish at your fingertips, perfect for any occasion. But our journey through Chicken Piccata is far from over.

Chapter 4: Lemon Herb Chicken Piccata

In this chapter, we'll elevate the classic Chicken Piccata by infusing it with the vibrant flavors of fresh herbs. Lemon Herb Chicken Piccata takes the traditional recipe to a new level of freshness and aroma. We'll explore how to create an herb-infused lemon sauce, learn about the art of pairing herbs with chicken, and discover exciting herb-marinated chicken variations that will delight your taste buds.

A Twist on the Classic with Fresh Herbs

Lemon Herb Chicken Piccata is a delightful twist on the classic recipe. The addition of fresh herbs not only adds layers of flavor but also enhances the visual appeal of the dish. Here's what you need to know to get started:

Herb Selection:

Choose a combination of fresh herbs that complement the bright and zesty flavors of Chicken Piccata. Popular choices include parsley, basil, tarragon, chives, and dill.

Herb-Infused Lemon Sauce:

To infuse the lemon-caper sauce with herbs, finely chop the selected herbs and stir them into the sauce just before serving. This adds a burst of freshness to every bite.

Pairing Herbs with Chicken

Pairing herbs with chicken requires a thoughtful approach to achieve harmony in flavors. Here are some herb-chicken pairings to consider:

Parsley: A versatile herb that pairs well with virtually any chicken dish. It adds a fresh, grassy flavor and a pop of green color to Lemon Herb Chicken Piccata.

Basil: Known for its sweet and slightly peppery flavor, basil is a classic herb for chicken. It complements the lemony sauce beautifully.

Tarragon: With its distinct anise-like flavor, tarragon adds a unique twist to the dish. Use it sparingly as it can be quite potent.

Chives: Chives have a mild onion flavor and provide a subtle kick to the sauce. They also make an excellent garnish.

Dill: Dill's delicate, feathery fronds bring a hint of licorice-like freshness to the dish. It pairs wonderfully with lemon.

Herb-Marinated Chicken Variations

To truly infuse the chicken with herb flavor, consider marinating the chicken cutlets before cooking. Here are some herb-marinated chicken variations to try:

Lemon-Parsley Marinated Chicken:

Create a marinade by combining fresh parsley, lemon juice, olive oil, garlic, and a pinch of salt. Marinate the chicken cutlets for at least 30 minutes before cooking.

Basil and Lemon Zest Marinated Chicken:

Marinate the chicken cutlets in a mixture of fresh basil leaves, lemon zest, garlic, olive oil, and a touch of red pepper flakes for a hint of heat.

Tarragon and White Wine Marinated Chicken:

Marinate the chicken cutlets in a mixture of tarragon leaves, white wine, lemon juice, and a bit of Dijon mustard for a tangy and aromatic twist.

Chive and Buttermilk Marinated Chicken:

Create a buttermilk-based marinade infused with chopped chives, lemon juice, and a dash of paprika. The buttermilk adds tenderness to the chicken.

By marinating the chicken with these herb-infused mixtures, you'll impart a deep herbaceous flavor to every bite, enhancing the Lemon Herb Chicken Piccata experience.

Lemon Herb Chicken Piccata Recipe
Ingredients:

- 4 boneless, skinless chicken cutlets (marinated as desired)
- Salt and freshly ground black pepper, to taste
- 1/2 cup all-purpose flour, for dredging
- 2 tablespoons olive oil
- 2 tablespoons unsalted butter
- 1/4 cup fresh lemon juice (about 2 lemons)
- 1/2 cup dry white wine
- 1/4 cup capers, drained and rinsed

- 1/4 cup chicken broth
- 2 cloves garlic, minced
- Fresh herb mix (parsley, basil, tarragon, chives, or dill), finely chopped for garnish

Step-by-Step Instructions:
Prepare the Chicken Cutlets:

1. If marinating, follow the instructions for your chosen herb-marinated chicken variation.
2. Season both sides of the chicken cutlets with salt and freshly ground black pepper.

Dredge in Flour:

1. Place the all-purpose flour in a shallow dish.
2. Dredge each chicken cutlet in the flour, shaking off any excess.

Pan-Fry the Chicken:

1. In a large skillet or frying pan, heat the olive oil and butter over medium-high heat.
2. Once the butter is foamy, add the chicken cutlets to the pan.
3. Cook for about 3-4 minutes on each side or until they are golden brown and cooked through.
4. Transfer the cooked chicken to a plate and cover with foil to keep warm.

Prepare the Lemon-Herb-Caper Sauce:

1. In the same skillet, add minced garlic and sauté for about 30 seconds until fragrant.
2. Deglaze the pan with the dry white wine, scraping up any browned bits from the bottom.

3. Add the fresh lemon juice and capers. Allow the sauce to simmer for about 5 minutes or until it has reduced slightly.

Infuse with Fresh Herbs:

Just before serving, stir in a generous amount of freshly chopped herbs into the sauce. This infuses the sauce with herbaceous flavor.

Combine Chicken and Sauce:

1. Return the cooked chicken cutlets to the skillet, turning them in the herb-infused lemon-caper sauce to coat evenly.
2. Simmer for an additional 2-3 minutes, allowing the chicken to absorb the flavors of the sauce.

Serve and Garnish:

1. Transfer the Lemon Herb Chicken Piccata to serving plates.
2. Garnish generously with additional chopped fresh herbs for a burst of freshness and vibrant color.

Lemon Herb Chicken Piccata is a delightful celebration of fresh herbs and zesty flavors. The aromatic infusion of herbs in both the sauce and the chicken cutlets takes this classic dish to a whole new level of culinary delight.

Chapter 5: Garlic Butter Chicken Piccata

In this chapter, we'll explore a luxurious variation of Chicken Piccata by adding richness and depth of flavor with the addition of garlic-infused butter. Garlic Butter Chicken Piccata takes the classic recipe to a whole new level of decadence. We'll provide you with a delectable garlic butter sauce recipe, walk you through creating a Garlic Lovers' Chicken Piccata, and even introduce an optional twist with Garlic Butter Shrimp Piccata for those who enjoy seafood.

Adding Richness with Garlic Butter

Garlic Butter Chicken Piccata is a delightful departure from the classic version, and it's perfect for garlic lovers. Here's how to achieve that rich, buttery goodness:

Garlic Butter Infusion:

Infuse the sauce with the robust flavors of garlic by adding it to the butter as it melts. This not only enhances the aroma but also adds depth to the sauce.

Butter Quality:

Use high-quality, unsalted butter for the best results. This allows you to control the saltiness of the dish.

Garlic Butter Sauce Recipe

Creating a luscious garlic butter sauce is at the heart of Garlic Butter Chicken Piccata. Here's a simple recipe:

Ingredients for Garlic Butter Sauce:

- 1/2 cup unsalted butter
- 6 cloves garlic, minced
- 1/4 cup fresh lemon juice (about 2 lemons)
- 1/2 cup dry white wine
- 1/4 cup capers, drained and rinsed

- 1/4 cup chicken broth

Instructions:

1. In a saucepan over medium heat, melt the unsalted butter.
2. Add the minced garlic and sauté for about 1-2 minutes until fragrant. Be careful not to let it brown.
3. Pour in the fresh lemon juice and dry white wine, stirring to combine.
4. Add the capers and chicken broth to the saucepan. Allow the mixture to simmer for about 5-7 minutes, or until the sauce has thickened slightly.
5. Once the sauce is ready, remove it from the heat and set it aside.

Garlic Lovers' Chicken Piccata
Ingredients for Garlic Butter Chicken Piccata:

- 4 boneless, skinless chicken cutlets
- Salt and freshly ground black pepper, to taste
- 1/2 cup all-purpose flour, for dredging
- 2 tablespoons olive oil
- Garlic Butter Sauce (as prepared above)
- Fresh parsley, chopped for garnish
- Lemon slices, for garnish

Step-by-Step Instructions:
Prepare the Chicken Cutlets:

1. Season both sides of the chicken cutlets with salt and freshly ground black pepper.
2. Dredge each chicken cutlet in the all-purpose flour, shaking off any excess.

Pan-Fry the Chicken:

1. In a large skillet or frying pan, heat the olive oil over medium-high heat.
2. Add the chicken cutlets to the pan and cook for about 3-4 minutes on each side or until they are golden brown and cooked through.
3. Transfer the cooked chicken to a plate and cover with foil to keep warm.

Combine Chicken and Garlic Butter Sauce:

1. Return the cooked chicken cutlets to the skillet.
2. Pour the prepared Garlic Butter Sauce over the chicken, coating them evenly.
3. Allow the chicken to simmer in the sauce for an additional 2-3 minutes to absorb the flavors.

Serve and Garnish:

1. Transfer the Garlic Butter Chicken Piccata to serving plates.
2. Garnish with chopped fresh parsley and lemon slices for a vibrant and aromatic finish.

Garlic Butter Shrimp Piccata (Optional)

For those who enjoy seafood, you can take this garlic butter infusion to the next level by preparing Garlic Butter Shrimp Piccata alongside or instead of the chicken. Simply substitute shrimp for chicken in the recipe, and you'll have a mouthwatering seafood version of this indulgent dish.

Chapter 6: Creamy Chicken Piccata

In this chapter, we'll explore delightful creamy variations of Chicken Piccata that take this classic dish to new heights of indulgence. Creamy Chicken Piccata offers a luxurious twist by introducing a velvety, lemony, and caper-infused cream sauce. We'll provide you with a delectable recipe for Creamy Lemon-Caper Sauce and guide you through creating two mouthwatering creamy variations: Creamy Mushroom Chicken Piccata and Creamy Spinach and Artichoke Chicken Piccata.

Introducing Creamy Variations

Creamy Chicken Piccata introduces a lush and velvety element to the traditional recipe. The addition of a creamy lemon-caper sauce enhances the overall richness of the dish, creating a comforting and decadent experience.

Creamy Lemon-Caper Sauce:

The key to a successful creamy lemon-caper sauce is to balance the flavors of creaminess, tartness from lemon, and the briny punch of capers.

Cream Variations:

Use heavy cream or half-and-half for the creaminess. You can adjust the amount to achieve your desired level of richness.

Creamy Lemon-Caper Sauce

Creating a creamy lemon-caper sauce is the foundation of Creamy Chicken Piccata. Here's a delicious recipe:

Ingredients for Creamy Lemon-Caper Sauce:

- 1/2 cup heavy cream or half-and-half
- 1/4 cup fresh lemon juice (about 2 lemons)
- 1/4 cup dry white wine
- 2 tablespoons unsalted butter

- 1/4 cup capers, drained and rinsed
- Salt and freshly ground black pepper, to taste
- Fresh parsley, chopped for garnish

Instructions:

1. In a saucepan over medium heat, melt the unsalted butter.
2. Pour in the fresh lemon juice and dry white wine, stirring to combine.
3. Add the capers to the saucepan and allow the mixture to simmer for about 3-4 minutes.
4. Reduce the heat to low and slowly stir in the heavy cream or half-and-half, whisking constantly until the sauce becomes smooth and creamy.
5. Season the sauce with salt and freshly ground black pepper to taste.
6. Once the sauce is ready, remove it from the heat and set it aside.

Creamy Mushroom Chicken Piccata
Ingredients for Creamy Mushroom Chicken Piccata:

- 4 boneless, skinless chicken cutlets
- Salt and freshly ground black pepper, to taste
- 1/2 cup all-purpose flour, for dredging
- 2 tablespoons olive oil
- Creamy Lemon-Caper Sauce (as prepared above)
- 8 oz. mushrooms, sliced
- Fresh parsley, chopped for garnish
- Lemon slices, for garnish

Step-by-Step Instructions:
Prepare the Chicken Cutlets:

1. Season both sides of the chicken cutlets with salt and freshly ground black pepper.
2. Dredge each chicken cutlet in the all-purpose flour, shaking off any excess.

Pan-Fry the Chicken:

1. In a large skillet or frying pan, heat the olive oil over medium-high heat.
2. Add the chicken cutlets to the pan and cook for about 3-4 minutes on each side or until they are golden brown and cooked through.
3. Transfer the cooked chicken to a plate and cover with foil to keep warm.

Sauté the Mushrooms:

In the same skillet, add the sliced mushrooms. Sauté them until they become tender and slightly browned, about 5-7 minutes.

Combine Chicken, Mushrooms, and Creamy Lemon-Caper Sauce:

1. Return the cooked chicken cutlets to the skillet, placing them on top of the sautéed mushrooms.
2. Pour the prepared Creamy Lemon-Caper Sauce over the chicken and mushrooms, allowing the flavors to meld together.
3. Simmer for an additional 2-3 minutes.

Serve and Garnish:

1. Transfer the Creamy Mushroom Chicken Piccata to serving plates.
2. Garnish with chopped fresh parsley and lemon slices for an

exquisite presentation.

Creamy Spinach and Artichoke Chicken Piccata
Ingredients for Creamy Spinach and Artichoke Chicken Piccata:

- 4 boneless, skinless chicken cutlets
- Salt and freshly ground black pepper, to taste
- 1/2 cup all-purpose flour, for dredging
- 2 tablespoons olive oil
- Creamy Lemon-Caper Sauce (as prepared above)
- 1 cup fresh baby spinach leaves
- 1/2 cup canned artichoke hearts, drained and quartered
- Fresh parsley, chopped for garnish
- Lemon slices, for garnish

Step-by-Step Instructions:
Prepare the Chicken Cutlets:

1. Season both sides of the chicken cutlets with salt and freshly ground black pepper.
2. Dredge each chicken cutlet in the all-purpose flour, shaking off any excess.

Pan-Fry the Chicken:

1. In a large skillet or frying pan, heat the olive oil over medium-high heat.
2. Add the chicken cutlets to the pan and cook for about 3-4 minutes on each side or until they are golden brown and cooked through.
3. Transfer the cooked chicken to a plate and cover with foil to keep warm.

Add Spinach and Artichokes:

1. In the same skillet, add the fresh baby spinach leaves and

       quartered artichoke hearts.

2. Sauté for about 2-3 minutes until the spinach wilts and the artichokes are heated through.

Combine Chicken, Spinach, Artichokes, and Creamy Lemon-Caper Sauce:

1. Return the cooked chicken cutlets to the skillet, arranging them on top of the spinach and artichokes.
2. Pour the prepared Creamy Lemon-Caper Sauce over the chicken, spinach, and artichokes, allowing the flavors to meld together.
3. Simmer for an additional 2-3 minutes.

Serve and Garnish:

1. Transfer the Creamy Spinach and Artichoke Chicken Piccata to serving plates.
2. Garnish with chopped fresh parsley and lemon slices for an elegant and appetizing finish.

Creamy Chicken Piccata variations offer a delightful departure from the traditional recipe, with velvety, lemony, and caper-infused cream sauces that make every bite truly indulgent.

Chapter 7: Mediterranean Chicken Piccata

In this chapter, we'll take a culinary journey to the Mediterranean and infuse the vibrant flavors of the region into Chicken Piccata. Mediterranean Chicken Piccata embraces the essence of Mediterranean cuisine with ingredients like olives, sun-dried tomatoes, and aromatic herbs. We'll provide you with two tantalizing Mediterranean-inspired Chicken Piccata recipes and suggest delightful Mediterranean sides to complement your dish.

Mediterranean Flavors and Ingredients

Mediterranean cuisine is known for its bold and harmonious flavors. To capture the essence of the Mediterranean in your Chicken Piccata, consider incorporating these key ingredients:

Olives:

Mediterranean olives, such as Kalamata or green olives, provide a briny and savory element to your dish.

Sun-Dried Tomatoes:

Sun-dried tomatoes infuse a rich, sweet-tart flavor that complements the lemony and caper-infused sauce.

Mediterranean Herbs:

Fresh herbs like oregano, basil, and thyme add depth and aroma to your Mediterranean Chicken Piccata.

Mediterranean Lemon-Herb Chicken Piccata

Ingredients for Mediterranean Lemon-Herb Chicken Piccata:

- 4 boneless, skinless chicken cutlets
- Salt and freshly ground black pepper, to taste
- 1/2 cup all-purpose flour, for dredging
- 2 tablespoons olive oil
- 1/4 cup fresh lemon juice (about 2 lemons)
- 1/2 cup dry white wine

- 1/4 cup Kalamata olives, pitted and sliced
- 1/4 cup sun-dried tomatoes, chopped
- 1/4 cup chicken broth
- 2 cloves garlic, minced
- Fresh Mediterranean herbs (oregano, basil, thyme), finely chopped for garnish
- Lemon slices, for garnish

Step-by-Step Instructions:
Prepare the Chicken Cutlets:

1. Season both sides of the chicken cutlets with salt and freshly ground black pepper.
2. Dredge each chicken cutlet in the all-purpose flour, shaking off any excess.

Pan-Fry the Chicken:

1. In a large skillet or frying pan, heat the olive oil over medium-high heat.
2. Add the chicken cutlets to the pan and cook for about 3-4 minutes on each side or until they are golden brown and cooked through.
3. Transfer the cooked chicken to a plate and cover with foil to keep warm.

Prepare the Mediterranean Lemon-Herb Sauce:

1. In the same skillet, add minced garlic and sauté for about 30 seconds until fragrant.
2. Deglaze the pan with the dry white wine, scraping up any browned bits from the bottom.
3. Add the fresh lemon juice, Kalamata olives, sun-dried tomatoes, and chicken broth.

4. Allow the sauce to simmer for about 5 minutes or until it has reduced slightly.

Combine Chicken and Mediterranean Sauce:

1. Return the cooked chicken cutlets to the skillet, turning them in the Mediterranean sauce to coat evenly.
2. Simmer for an additional 2-3 minutes, allowing the chicken to absorb the flavors.

Serve and Garnish:

1. Transfer the Mediterranean Lemon-Herb Chicken Piccata to serving plates.
2. Garnish with a generous sprinkle of freshly chopped Mediterranean herbs and lemon slices for a burst of Mediterranean freshness.

Olive and Sun-Dried Tomato Chicken Piccata
Ingredients for Olive and Sun-Dried Tomato Chicken Piccata:

- 4 boneless, skinless chicken cutlets
- Salt and freshly ground black pepper, to taste
- 1/2 cup all-purpose flour, for dredging
- 2 tablespoons olive oil
- 1/4 cup fresh lemon juice (about 2 lemons)
- 1/2 cup dry white wine
- 1/4 cup Kalamata olives, pitted and sliced
- 1/4 cup sun-dried tomatoes, chopped
- 1/4 cup chicken broth
- Fresh parsley, chopped for garnish
- Lemon slices, for garnish

Step-by-Step Instructions:
Prepare the Chicken Cutlets:

1. Season both sides of the chicken cutlets with salt and freshly ground black pepper.
2. Dredge each chicken cutlet in the all-purpose flour, shaking off any excess.

Pan-Fry the Chicken:

1. In a large skillet or frying pan, heat the olive oil over medium-high heat.
2. Add the chicken cutlets to the pan and cook for about 3-4 minutes on each side or until they are golden brown and cooked through.
3. Transfer the cooked chicken to a plate and cover with foil to keep warm.

Prepare the Olive and Sun-Dried Tomato Sauce:
In the same skillet, add the fresh lemon juice, dry white wine, Kalamata olives, sun-dried tomatoes, and chicken broth. Allow the sauce to simmer for about 5 minutes or until it has reduced slightly.

Combine Chicken and Mediterranean Sauce:

1. Return the cooked chicken cutlets to the skillet, turning them in the olive and sun-dried tomato sauce to coat evenly.
2. Simmer for an additional 2-3 minutes, allowing the chicken to absorb the flavors.

Serve and Garnish:

1. Transfer the Olive and Sun-Dried Tomato Chicken Piccata to serving plates.
2. Garnish with chopped fresh parsley and lemon slices for a Mediterranean-inspired presentation.

Serving with Mediterranean Sides
Enhance your Mediterranean Chicken Piccata experience by serving it with Mediterranean-inspired sides. Here are some ideas:

Greek Salad: A refreshing Greek salad with cucumbers, tomatoes, red onions, feta cheese, and a simple vinaigrette.

Couscous: Fluffy and aromatic couscous cooked with herbs and lemon zest.

Roasted Vegetables: Mediterranean-style roasted vegetables, such as bell peppers, zucchini, and eggplant, seasoned with olive oil, garlic, and herbs.

Hummus: Creamy hummus served with warm pita bread or fresh vegetable sticks.

Tzatziki: A cooling cucumber and yogurt tzatziki sauce for dipping.

Enjoy the Flavors of the Mediterranean

Mediterranean Chicken Piccata brings the vibrant flavors of the Mediterranean to your plate. Whether you choose the Mediterranean Lemon-Herb version or the Olive and Sun-Dried Tomato variation, you're in for a culinary journey that celebrates the rich and diverse tastes of the Mediterranean region.

Chapter 8: Spicy Cajun Chicken Piccata

In this chapter, we'll introduce a fiery twist to the classic Chicken Piccata with the bold flavors of Cajun cuisine. Spicy Cajun Chicken Piccata combines the zesty and spicy Cajun spice blend with the traditional lemon-caper sauce, creating a tantalizing fusion of flavors. We'll provide you with a homemade Cajun Spice Blend recipe, guide you through preparing Spicy Cajun Chicken Piccata, and even introduce a delightful combo with Cajun Shrimp and Chicken Piccata.

Adding Heat with Cajun Spices

Cajun cuisine is renowned for its bold and spicy flavors, and it's the perfect partner to elevate your Chicken Piccata. To add heat and depth, consider using these key Cajun spices and ingredients:

Cajun Spice Blend:

Create a homemade Cajun spice blend featuring paprika, cayenne pepper, garlic powder, onion powder, thyme, oregano, and other aromatic spices.

Cajun Heat:

Incorporate cayenne pepper, hot sauce, or chili flakes to bring the signature Cajun heat to your dish.

Cajun Spice Blend Recipe

Creating your own Cajun spice blend allows you to control the level of spiciness and flavor. Here's a homemade Cajun Spice Blend recipe:

Ingredients for Cajun Spice Blend:

- 2 tablespoons paprika
- 1 tablespoon garlic powder
- 1 tablespoon onion powder
- 1 tablespoon dried oregano
- 1 tablespoon dried thyme

- 1 teaspoon cayenne pepper (adjust to taste)
- 1 teaspoon white pepper
- 1 teaspoon black pepper
- 1 teaspoon salt

Instructions:

1. In a small bowl, combine all the spices and herbs: paprika, garlic powder, onion powder, dried oregano, dried thyme, cayenne pepper, white pepper, black pepper, and salt.
2. Mix thoroughly until all the ingredients are well combined.
3. Store the Cajun Spice Blend in an airtight container in a cool, dry place for future use.

Spicy Cajun Chicken Piccata
Ingredients for Spicy Cajun Chicken Piccata:

- 4 boneless, skinless chicken cutlets
- Salt and Cajun Spice Blend, to taste
- 1/2 cup all-purpose flour, for dredging
- 2 tablespoons olive oil
- 2 tablespoons unsalted butter
- 1/4 cup fresh lemon juice (about 2 lemons)
- 1/2 cup dry white wine
- 1/4 cup capers, drained and rinsed
- 1/4 cup chicken broth
- 2 cloves garlic, minced
- Fresh parsley, chopped for garnish
- Lemon slices, for garnish

Step-by-Step Instructions:
Season with Cajun Spice Blend:

Season both sides of the chicken cutlets with salt and a generous amount of Cajun Spice Blend. Adjust the spiciness to your preference.

Dredge in Flour:

1. Place the all-purpose flour in a shallow dish.
2. Dredge each seasoned chicken cutlet in the flour, shaking off any excess.

Pan-Fry the Chicken:

1. In a large skillet or frying pan, heat the olive oil and unsalted butter over medium-high heat.
2. Once the butter is foamy, add the chicken cutlets to the pan.
3. Cook for about 3-4 minutes on each side or until they are golden brown and cooked through.
4. Transfer the cooked chicken to a plate and cover with foil to keep warm.

Prepare the Lemon-Caper Sauce:

In the same skillet, add minced garlic and sauté for about 30 seconds until fragrant.

Deglaze and Add Flavor:

Deglaze the pan with the dry white wine, scraping up any browned bits from the bottom.

Add the fresh lemon juice, capers, and chicken broth. Allow the sauce to simmer for about 5 minutes or until it has reduced slightly.

Combine Chicken and Spicy Lemon-Caper Sauce:

Return the cooked chicken cutlets to the skillet, turning them in the spicy lemon-caper sauce to coat evenly.

Simmer for an additional 2-3 minutes, allowing the chicken to absorb the bold flavors.

Serve and Garnish:

Transfer the Spicy Cajun Chicken Piccata to serving plates.

Garnish with chopped fresh parsley and lemon slices for an extra burst of flavor and color.

Cajun Shrimp and Chicken Piccata
Ingredients for Cajun Shrimp and Chicken Piccata:

- 2 boneless, skinless chicken breasts, cut into thin strips
- 8 large shrimp, peeled and deveined
- Salt and Cajun Spice Blend, to taste
- 1/2 cup all-purpose flour, for dredging
- 2 tablespoons olive oil
- 2 tablespoons unsalted butter
- 1/4 cup fresh lemon juice (about 2 lemons)
- 1/2 cup dry white wine
- 1/4 cup capers, drained and rinsed
- 1/4 cup chicken broth
- 2 cloves garlic, minced
- Fresh parsley, chopped for garnish
- Lemon slices, for garnish

Step-by-Step Instructions:
Season Chicken and Shrimp:

Season the chicken strips and shrimp with salt and Cajun Spice Blend, ensuring they are well coated.

Dredge in Flour:

Place the all-purpose flour in a shallow dish.

Dredge both the seasoned chicken strips and shrimp in the flour, shaking off any excess.

Pan-Fry Chicken and Shrimp:

In a large skillet or frying pan, heat the olive oil and unsalted butter over medium-high heat.

Add the chicken strips and shrimp to the pan.

Cook the chicken for about 2-3 minutes per side and the shrimp for about 1-2 minutes per side, or until they are cooked through and golden brown.

Transfer the cooked chicken and shrimp to a plate and cover with foil to keep warm.

Prepare the Lemon-Caper Sauce:

In the same skillet, add minced garlic and sauté for about 30 seconds until fragrant.

Deglaze and Add Flavor:

Deglaze the pan with the dry white wine, scraping up any browned bits from the bottom.

Add the fresh lemon juice, capers, and chicken broth. Allow the sauce to simmer for about 5 minutes or until it has reduced slightly.

Combine Chicken, Shrimp, and Spicy Lemon-Caper Sauce:

Return the cooked chicken strips and shrimp to the skillet, turning them in the spicy lemon-caper sauce to coat evenly.

Simmer for an additional 2-3 minutes, allowing the protein to absorb the bold flavors.

Serve and Garnish:

Transfer the Cajun Shrimp and Chicken Piccata to serving plates.

Garnish with chopped fresh parsley and lemon slices for a colorful and spicy presentation.

A Spicy Twist on a Classic

Spicy Cajun Chicken Piccata brings the fiery and bold flavors of Cajun cuisine to this beloved Italian classic. Whether you choose the chicken-only version or the tantalizing combination of chicken and shrimp, your taste buds are in for a thrilling experience.

Chapter 9: Parmesan-Crusted Chicken Piccata

In this chapter, we're putting a cheesy twist on the classic Chicken Piccata with Parmesan-Crusted Chicken Piccata. This delightful variation combines the zesty flavors of Chicken Piccata with a crispy Parmesan crust that adds a rich and savory dimension to the dish. We'll guide you on how to create the perfect Parmesan crust, provide you with a mouthwatering recipe for Parmesan-Crusted Chicken Piccata, and offer serving suggestions and pairings to complete your meal.

A Cheesy Twist on Chicken Piccata

Parmesan-Crusted Chicken Piccata takes the classic recipe to a whole new level of indulgence by adding a layer of crispy, golden-brown Parmesan cheese crust. The combination of the tangy lemon-caper sauce and the cheesy crust creates a harmonious and delectable balance of flavors and textures.

Key Ingredient: Parmesan Cheese

High-quality Parmesan cheese is essential for achieving the perfect Parmesan crust. Look for Parmigiano-Reggiano or Pecorino Romano for an authentic and nutty flavor.

How to Create the Perfect Parmesan Crust

Creating a flawless Parmesan crust requires attention to detail. Here's how to achieve the perfect crust:

Breading Process:

1. Dredge the seasoned chicken cutlets in flour to create a dry surface.
2. Dip them in beaten eggs to allow the Parmesan to adhere.
3. Coat the chicken generously with a mixture of grated Parmesan cheese and breadcrumbs.

Searing Technique:

Use a combination of olive oil and butter for pan-frying the chicken. This helps in achieving a crispy and flavorful crust.

Parmesan-Crusted Chicken Piccata Recipe

Ingredients for Parmesan-Crusted Chicken Piccata:

- 4 boneless, skinless chicken cutlets
- Salt and freshly ground black pepper, to taste
- 1/2 cup all-purpose flour, for dredging
- 2 large eggs, beaten
- 1 cup grated Parmesan cheese
- 1/2 cup breadcrumbs
- 2 tablespoons olive oil
- 2 tablespoons unsalted butter
- 1/4 cup fresh lemon juice (about 2 lemons)
- 1/2 cup dry white wine
- 1/4 cup capers, drained and rinsed
- 1/4 cup chicken broth
- Fresh parsley, chopped for garnish
- Lemon slices, for garnish

Step-by-Step Instructions:

Season and Dredge Chicken Cutlets:

1. Season both sides of the chicken cutlets with salt and freshly ground black pepper.
2. Dredge each seasoned chicken cutlet in the all-purpose flour, shaking off any excess.

Create the Parmesan Crust:

1. In a shallow dish, combine grated Parmesan cheese and breadcrumbs.
2. Dip each flour-coated chicken cutlet into the beaten eggs, ensuring it's fully coated.

3. Coat the chicken generously with the Parmesan and breadcrumb mixture, pressing gently to adhere.

Pan-Fry the Parmesan-Crusted Chicken:

1. In a large skillet or frying pan, heat the olive oil and unsalted butter over medium-high heat.
2. Add the Parmesan-crusted chicken cutlets to the pan.
3. Cook for about 3-4 minutes on each side or until they are golden brown and the cheese crust is crispy.
4. Transfer the cooked chicken to a plate and cover with foil to keep warm.

Prepare the Lemon-Caper Sauce:

1. In the same skillet, add fresh lemon juice and deglaze the pan.
2. Pour in the dry white wine and add the capers and chicken broth.
3. Allow the sauce to simmer for about 5 minutes or until it has reduced slightly.

Combine Parmesan-Crusted Chicken with Lemon-Caper Sauce:

1. Return the cooked Parmesan-crusted chicken cutlets to the skillet, turning them in the lemon-caper sauce to coat evenly.
2. Simmer for an additional 2-3 minutes to infuse the flavors.

Serve and Garnish:

1. Transfer the Parmesan-Crusted Chicken Piccata to serving plates.
2. Garnish with chopped fresh parsley and lemon slices for a visually appealing and flavorful finish.

Serving Suggestions and Pairings

Parmesan-Crusted Chicken Piccata pairs beautifully with a variety of side dishes. Here are some serving suggestions to complete your meal:

Creamy Mashed Potatoes: Silky-smooth mashed potatoes complement the rich and crispy chicken.

Steamed Asparagus: A side of steamed asparagus drizzled with lemon butter adds freshness and color to your plate.

Lemon-Herb Risotto: Creamy lemon-herb risotto makes for a luxurious and flavorful accompaniment.

Mixed Green Salad: A light and refreshing mixed green salad with a lemon vinaigrette provides balance and contrast.

Garlic Bread: Serve with warm garlic bread for an extra touch of indulgence.

Enjoy the Crispy, Cheesy Goodness

Parmesan-Crusted Chicken Piccata offers a delightful combination of crispy, cheesy goodness and the zesty flavors of Chicken Piccata. It's a dish that's sure to impress your family and guests with its rich and savory profile.

Chapter 10: Pesto Chicken Piccata

In this chapter, we're infusing the vibrant and fresh flavors of pesto into the classic Chicken Piccata to create Pesto Chicken Piccata. This delightful twist combines the herbal and nutty notes of pesto with the zesty lemon-caper sauce, resulting in a harmonious fusion of flavors. We'll guide you on how to prepare homemade pesto sauce, provide a delicious recipe for Pesto-Marinated Chicken Piccata, and suggest serving it over Pesto Pasta for a complete and satisfying meal.

Incorporating Pesto for a Fresh Flavor

Pesto is a versatile sauce originating from Italy, traditionally made with fresh basil, pine nuts, Parmesan cheese, garlic, and olive oil. It adds a burst of fresh and herbaceous flavor to your Chicken Piccata. To make the most of pesto, consider these key ingredients and techniques:

Homemade Pesto Sauce:

Creating your own pesto sauce ensures the freshest and most vibrant flavors. You can adjust the ingredients to your taste preferences.

Marinating Chicken:

Marinating the chicken in pesto sauce before cooking allows the flavors to penetrate the meat and infuse it with herbal and nutty notes.

Homemade Pesto Sauce

Here's a simple recipe to make homemade pesto sauce:

Ingredients for Homemade Pesto Sauce:

1. 2 cups fresh basil leaves, packed
2. 1/2 cup grated Parmesan cheese
3. 1/2 cup pine nuts (or walnuts for a different twist)
4. 3 cloves garlic, minced
5. 1/2 cup extra-virgin olive oil
6. Salt and freshly ground black pepper, to taste

Instructions:

1. In a food processor, combine the fresh basil leaves, grated Parmesan cheese, pine nuts (or walnuts), and minced garlic.
2. Pulse the ingredients until they are finely chopped.
3. With the food processor running, slowly drizzle in the extra-virgin olive oil until the pesto reaches your desired consistency.
4. Season with salt and freshly ground black pepper to taste. Adjust the flavors as needed.
5. Transfer the homemade pesto sauce to an airtight container and refrigerate until ready to use.

Pesto-Marinated Chicken Piccata
Ingredients for Pesto-Marinated Chicken Piccata:

- 4 boneless, skinless chicken cutlets
- Salt and freshly ground black pepper, to taste
- 1/2 cup pesto sauce (homemade or store-bought)
- 1/2 cup all-purpose flour, for dredging
- 2 tablespoons olive oil
- 2 tablespoons unsalted butter
- 1/4 cup fresh lemon juice (about 2 lemons)
- 1/2 cup dry white wine
- 1/4 cup capers, drained and rinsed
- 1/4 cup chicken broth
- Fresh basil leaves, for garnish
- Lemon slices, for garnish

Step-by-Step Instructions:
Marinate the Chicken:

1. Season both sides of the chicken cutlets with salt and freshly ground black pepper.
2. Coat the chicken cutlets with pesto sauce, ensuring they are fully marinated.
3. Refrigerate for at least 30 minutes to allow the flavors to infuse.

Dredge in Flour:

1. Place the all-purpose flour in a shallow dish.
2. Dredge each pesto-marinated chicken cutlet in the flour, shaking off any excess.

Pan-Fry the Chicken:

1. In a large skillet or frying pan, heat the olive oil and unsalted butter over medium-high heat.
2. Add the pesto-marinated chicken cutlets to the pan.
3. Cook for about 3-4 minutes on each side or until they are golden brown and cooked through.
4. Transfer the cooked chicken to a plate and cover with foil to keep warm.

Prepare the Lemon-Caper Sauce:

1. In the same skillet, add fresh lemon juice and deglaze the pan.
2. Pour in the dry white wine and add the capers and chicken broth. Allow the sauce to simmer for about 5 minutes or until it has reduced slightly.

Combine Chicken with Lemon-Caper Sauce:

1. Return the cooked pesto-marinated chicken cutlets to the skillet, turning them in the lemon-caper sauce to coat evenly.
2. Simmer for an additional 2-3 minutes to meld the flavors.

Serve and Garnish:

1. Transfer the Pesto-Marinated Chicken Piccata to serving plates.
2. Garnish with fresh basil leaves and lemon slices for a burst of freshness and visual appeal.

Pesto Pasta and Chicken Piccata

For a complete and satisfying meal, serve your Pesto Chicken Piccata over a bed of cooked pasta tossed with additional pesto sauce. It creates a harmonious fusion of flavors and textures that will delight your taste buds.

Fresh and Flavorful Fusion

Pesto Chicken Piccata brings together the best of two culinary worlds - the freshness of pesto and the zesty allure of Chicken Piccata. Whether you serve it with pasta or enjoy it on its own, this dish offers a delightful and flavorful fusion.

Chapter 11: Sheet Pan Chicken Piccata

In this chapter, we're simplifying the cooking process and minimizing cleanup with Sheet Pan Chicken Piccata. This easy one-pan recipe allows you to enjoy the classic flavors of Chicken Piccata without the hassle of multiple pots and pans. We'll guide you through preparing Sheet Pan Chicken Piccata, creating a flavorful roasted vegetable medley to accompany it, and explore how this dish is the perfect solution for a quick weeknight dinner.

Easy One-Pan Chicken Piccata

Sheet Pan Chicken Piccata is a convenient and efficient way to prepare this beloved dish. By using a single sheet pan for both the chicken and vegetables, you'll save time and effort in the kitchen while still savoring the flavors of Chicken Piccata.

Key Advantage: Minimal Cleanup

With only one sheet pan to clean, this recipe is a weeknight dinner hero.

Preparing Sheet Pan Chicken Piccata
Here's how to make Sheet Pan Chicken Piccata:
Ingredients for Sheet Pan Chicken Piccata:
For the Chicken:

- 4 boneless, skinless chicken breasts
- Salt and freshly ground black pepper, to taste
- 1/2 cup all-purpose flour, for dredging
- 2 tablespoons olive oil
- For the Lemon-Caper Sauce:
- 1/4 cup unsalted butter, melted
- 1/4 cup fresh lemon juice (about 2 lemons)
- 1/4 cup dry white wine
- 1/4 cup capers, drained and rinsed
- 1/4 cup chicken broth

- 2 cloves garlic, minced
- For the Roasted Vegetable Medley:
- 2 cups assorted vegetables (e.g., bell peppers, zucchini, cherry tomatoes)
- 2 tablespoons olive oil
- Salt and freshly ground black pepper, to taste
- Fresh parsley, chopped for garnish
- Lemon slices, for garnish

Step-by-Step Instructions:
Preheat the Oven:

1. Preheat your oven to 400°F (200°C).

Season and Dredge the Chicken:

1. Season both sides of the chicken breasts with salt and freshly ground black pepper.
2. Dredge each chicken breast in the all-purpose flour, shaking off any excess.

Arrange Chicken on a Sheet Pan:

1. Place the chicken breasts on a sheet pan lined with parchment paper or aluminum foil.

Drizzle with Olive Oil:

1. Drizzle olive oil over the chicken breasts.

Bake the Chicken:

1. Bake in the preheated oven for about 20-25 minutes or until the chicken is cooked through and golden brown.

Prepare the Lemon-Caper Sauce:

1. In a small saucepan, combine melted unsalted butter, fresh lemon juice, dry white wine, capers, chicken broth, and minced garlic.
2. Heat the sauce over medium heat until it simmers, then reduce the heat and simmer for about 5 minutes until the sauce has slightly thickened.

Roast the Vegetables:

1. While the chicken is baking, toss the assorted vegetables with olive oil, salt, and freshly ground black pepper.
2. Arrange the seasoned vegetables on the same sheet pan around the chicken during the last 10-15 minutes of baking. Roast until the vegetables are tender and slightly caramelized.

Combine Chicken, Vegetables, and Lemon-Caper Sauce:

1. Once the chicken and vegetables are done, pour the prepared lemon-caper sauce over the chicken and drizzle some over the roasted vegetables.

Serve and Garnish:

Transfer the Sheet Pan Chicken Piccata and the roasted vegetable medley to serving plates.

Garnish with chopped fresh parsley and lemon slices for a delightful presentation.

A Quick Weeknight Dinner Solution

Sheet Pan Chicken Piccata is the ideal solution for busy weeknights when you want a delicious and satisfying meal without the fuss of multiple dishes. It's a practical and flavorful way to enjoy the classic flavors of Chicken Piccata while keeping the cooking and cleanup simple.

Chapter 12: Slow Cooker Chicken Piccata

In this chapter, we're taking the effort out of cooking Chicken Piccata with the convenient and time-saving Slow Cooker Chicken Piccata recipe. You can enjoy all the flavors of this classic dish with minimal hands-on cooking. We'll provide you with an effortless Slow Cooker Chicken Piccata recipe, share time-saving tips, and suggest serving it over rice or pasta for a complete and comforting meal.

Effortless Chicken Piccata in the Slow Cooker

Slow Cooker Chicken Piccata is a hassle-free way to enjoy the flavors of this beloved dish without the need for constant attention. The slow cooker does the work for you, allowing you to come home to a delicious, ready-to-eat meal.

Key Advantage: Time-Saving Convenience

The slow cooker allows you to prepare a gourmet meal with minimal effort, making it perfect for busy days.

Slow Cooker Chicken Piccata Recipe

Here's how to make Slow Cooker Chicken Piccata:

Ingredients for Slow Cooker Chicken Piccata:

- 4 boneless, skinless chicken breasts
- Salt and freshly ground black pepper, to taste
- 1/2 cup all-purpose flour, for dredging
- 2 tablespoons olive oil
- 1/4 cup fresh lemon juice (about 2 lemons)
- 1/4 cup dry white wine
- 1/4 cup capers, drained and rinsed
- 1/4 cup chicken broth
- 2 cloves garlic, minced
- 2 tablespoons unsalted butter
- Fresh parsley, chopped for garnish
- Lemon slices, for garnish

Step-by-Step Instructions:
Season and Dredge the Chicken:

1. Season both sides of the chicken breasts with salt and freshly ground black pepper.
2. Dredge each chicken breast in the all-purpose flour, shaking off any excess.

Preheat a Skillet:

1. Heat a large skillet over medium-high heat and add olive oil.

Sear the Chicken:

1. Once the oil is hot, sear the chicken breasts for about 2-3 minutes on each side or until they are golden brown. This step is to create a nice crust on the chicken; it doesn't need to cook through.

Transfer to Slow Cooker:

1. Transfer the seared chicken breasts to the slow cooker.

Prepare the Lemon-Caper Sauce:

1. In a small saucepan, combine fresh lemon juice, dry white wine, capers, chicken broth, minced garlic, and unsalted butter.
2. Heat the sauce over medium heat until it simmers, then reduce the heat and simmer for about 5 minutes until the sauce has slightly thickened.

Pour Sauce Over Chicken:

1. Pour the prepared lemon-caper sauce over the chicken in the

slow cooker.

Cook in the Slow Cooker:

1. Cover the slow cooker and cook on low for 4-5 hours or until the chicken is tender and cooked through.

Serve and Garnish:

1. Transfer the Slow Cooker Chicken Piccata to serving plates.
2. Garnish with chopped fresh parsley and lemon slices for an appealing and flavorful finish.

Time-Saving Tips

Here are some time-saving tips to make Slow Cooker Chicken Piccata even more convenient:

Prep Ahead: Prepare the lemon-caper sauce and dredge the chicken in flour the night before. Store them separately in the refrigerator until you're ready to cook.

Use Chicken Cutlets: opt for chicken cutlets instead of whole chicken breasts for quicker cooking.

Serving Over Rice or Pasta

Slow Cooker Chicken Piccata pairs wonderfully with rice or pasta. The choice is yours! The flavorful lemon-caper sauce complements both options, creating a satisfying and comforting meal.

Effortless Gourmet Dining

Slow Cooker Chicken Piccata offers the perfect balance of convenience and gourmet dining. It's a fantastic way to enjoy the classic flavors of Chicken Piccata with minimal hands-on cooking.

Chapter 13: Healthy and Light Chicken Piccata

In this chapter, we're focusing on creating healthier and lighter variations of Chicken Piccata. We'll explore options like baked or grilled chicken, a lighter lemon-caper sauce, and suggest nutritious sides to create a balanced meal that's both delicious and mindful of your health.

Healthier Variations of Chicken Piccata

Enjoying a healthy and light Chicken Piccata doesn't mean sacrificing flavor. By making a few adjustments, you can create a dish that's lower in calories and saturated fats while still preserving the delightful taste of this classic Italian favorite.

Key Principles:

- Reducing butter and using heart-healthy olive oil.

- Opting for leaner cooking methods like baking or grilling.

- Creating a lighter lemon-caper sauce with reduced sodium.

Baked or Grilled Chicken Options

For a healthier twist on Chicken Piccata, consider baking or grilling the chicken instead of pan-frying. These methods significantly reduce the amount of oil used while still delivering a delicious result.

Baked Chicken:

Baking the chicken in the oven is a simple and effective way to achieve a healthier dish. It requires less oil and ensures even cooking.

Grilled Chicken:

Grilling adds a smoky flavor to the chicken without the need for excess oil.

Marinating the chicken in herbs and lemon juice before grilling enhances its taste.

Light Lemon-Caper Sauce

Creating a lighter lemon-caper sauce is key to keeping the dish healthy. Here's how to make a lighter version:

Ingredients for Light Lemon-Caper Sauce:

- 2 tablespoons olive oil
- 1/4 cup fresh lemon juice (about 2 lemons)
- 1/4 cup dry white wine (or low-sodium chicken broth)
- 2 tablespoons capers, drained and rinsed
- 2 cloves garlic, minced
- 1 tablespoon cornstarch (optional, for thickening)
- Salt and freshly ground black pepper, to taste

Instructions:

Prepare the Lemon-Caper Sauce:

1. In a small saucepan, heat olive oil over medium heat.
2. Add minced garlic and sauté for about 30 seconds until fragrant.

Create the Sauce:

1. Pour in fresh lemon juice, dry white wine (or chicken broth), and capers.
2. If you prefer a thicker sauce, dissolve 1 tablespoon of cornstarch in a small amount of water and add it to the sauce.

Simmer and Season:

1. Allow the sauce to simmer for about 5-7 minutes until it has reduced and thickened slightly.
2. Season with salt and freshly ground black pepper to taste. Adjust flavors as needed.

Sides for a Balanced Meal

Completing your healthy and light Chicken Piccata meal with nutritious sides is essential. Consider serving it with the following options:

Steamed Asparagus: A side of steamed asparagus adds a vibrant and healthy element to your plate.

Quinoa Salad: A quinoa salad with fresh vegetables and a lemon vinaigrette complements the lightness of the dish.

Mixed Greens: A simple mixed green salad with a light dressing adds freshness and color.

Brown Rice: Serve the Chicken Piccata over brown rice for added fiber and nutrients.

Roasted Vegetables: A medley of roasted vegetables, such as bell peppers, zucchini, and carrots, provides a satisfying and healthy accompaniment.

Savoring Flavorful Health

Healthy and Light Chicken Piccata offers a mindful approach to enjoying this classic dish. By making small changes to the ingredients and cooking methods, you can savor the flavors while prioritizing your health and well-being.

Chapter 14: Vegetarian Chicken Piccata (with Meat Alternatives)

In this chapter, we're exploring a delicious vegetarian twist on Chicken Piccata. You'll discover how to create a meatless "chicken" using plant-based alternatives, prepare a vegetarian lemon-caper sauce, and find vegan and vegetarian side dish options to complete your plant-based meal.

Vegetarian and Meatless Alternatives

Enjoying a vegetarian version of Chicken Piccata is both satisfying and environmentally friendly. There are various plant-based "chicken" alternatives available that mimic the taste and texture of poultry. These alternatives include products made from tofu, tempeh, seitan, and plant-based protein blends.

Key Considerations:

- Look for meatless alternatives that are suitable for your dietary preferences, such as vegan or vegetarian.

- Experiment with different plant-based "chicken" options to find the one that best suits your taste.

Preparing Plant-Based "Chicken"

Creating meatless "chicken" for your Vegetarian Chicken Piccata is straightforward and customizable. Here's a basic method:

Ingredients for Plant-Based "Chicken":

- 4 pieces of meatless chicken alternative (tofu, tempeh, seitan, etc.)
- Salt and freshly ground black pepper, to taste
- 1/2 cup all-purpose flour, for dredging
- 2 tablespoons olive oil

Step-by-Step Instructions:
Slice and Season:

1. Slice the plant-based "chicken" alternative into cutlet-sized pieces.
2. Season both sides with salt and freshly ground black pepper.

Dredge in Flour:

1. Dredge each piece in all-purpose flour, shaking off any excess.

Preheat a Skillet:

1. Heat a large skillet over medium-high heat and add olive oil.

Sear the "Chicken:"

Once the oil is hot, sear the plant-based "chicken" pieces for about 2-3 minutes on each side or until they are golden brown. This step is to create a nice crust; the "chicken" does not need to cook through.

Vegetarian Lemon-Caper Sauce

To maintain the flavors of Chicken Piccata in a vegetarian version, create a vegetarian lemon-caper sauce. Here's how:

Ingredients for Vegetarian Lemon-Caper Sauce:

- 2 tablespoons olive oil
- 1/4 cup fresh lemon juice (about 2 lemons)
- 1/4 cup dry white wine (or vegetable broth)
- 2 tablespoons capers, drained and rinsed
- 2 cloves garlic, minced
- 1 tablespoon cornstarch (optional, for thickening)
- Salt and freshly ground black pepper, to taste

Instructions:
Prepare the Vegetarian Lemon-Caper Sauce:

1. In a small saucepan, heat olive oil over medium heat.
2. Add minced garlic and sauté for about 30 seconds until fragrant.

Create the Sauce:

1. Pour in fresh lemon juice, dry white wine (or vegetable broth), and capers.
2. If you prefer a thicker sauce, dissolve 1 tablespoon of cornstarch in a small amount of water and add it to the sauce.

Simmer and Season:

1. Allow the sauce to simmer for about 5-7 minutes until it has

reduced and thickened slightly.

2. Season with salt and freshly ground black pepper to taste. Adjust flavors as needed.

Vegan and Vegetarian Side Dishes

Complete your Vegetarian Chicken Piccata meal with delicious vegan and vegetarian side dishes. Here are some options:

Vegan Garlic Mashed Potatoes: Creamy mashed potatoes made with plant-based butter and dairy-free milk.

Steamed Broccoli: A side of steamed broccoli adds freshness and nutrients to your plate.

Vegan Risotto: Creamy vegan risotto infused with lemon and herbs.

Mixed Green Salad: A vegan salad with mixed greens, cherry tomatoes, and a lemon vinaigrette dressing.

Vegan Garlic Bread: Serve with warm vegan garlic bread for a satisfying touch.

Savoring Plant-Based Delight

Vegetarian Chicken Piccata with meat alternatives offers a delightful and compassionate twist on the classic dish. Whether you're vegan, vegetarian, or simply looking to reduce your meat consumption, this dish is a flavorful and satisfying choice.

Chapter 15: Gluten-Free Chicken Piccata

In this chapter, we're catering to gluten-free diets by offering a delicious and gluten-free version of Chicken Piccata. You'll discover how to create a gluten-free breading for your chicken, prepare a gluten-free lemon-caper sauce, and find recommendations for gluten-free pasta to complete your meal.

Catering to Gluten-Free Diets

Enjoying a gluten-free version of Chicken Piccata is a great way to accommodate dietary restrictions while savoring the flavors of this classic dish. Whether you have celiac disease or prefer gluten-free options, you can still enjoy a delicious and safe meal.

Key Considerations:

1. Use gluten-free ingredients for breading, sauces, and pasta.
2. Ensure that all utensils and cookware are thoroughly cleaned to prevent cross-contamination.

Gluten-Free Breading Options

Creating a gluten-free breading for your chicken is easy with the right ingredients. Here are some gluten-free options for breading:

Gluten-Free Flours:

Use gluten-free flours like rice flour, cornmeal, or a gluten-free all-purpose flour blend for dredging your chicken.

Gluten-Free Breadcrumbs:

Purchase certified gluten-free breadcrumbs or make your own by processing gluten-free bread into crumbs.

Gluten-Free Alternatives:

Crushed gluten-free crackers, rice cereal, or even crushed gluten-free potato chips can add a delightful crunch to your chicken.

Gluten-Free Lemon-Caper Sauce

To maintain the authenticity of Chicken Piccata while keeping it gluten-free, create a gluten-free lemon-caper sauce. Here's how:

Ingredients for Gluten-Free Lemon-Caper Sauce:

- 2 tablespoons olive oil
- 1/4 cup fresh lemon juice (about 2 lemons)
- 1/4 cup dry white wine (ensure it's gluten-free)
- 2 tablespoons capers, drained and rinsed
- 2 cloves garlic, minced
- 1 tablespoon cornstarch (or gluten-free flour)
- Salt and freshly ground black pepper, to taste

Instructions:

1. Prepare the Gluten-Free Lemon-Caper Sauce:
2. In a small saucepan, heat olive oil over medium heat.
3. Add minced garlic and sauté for about 30 seconds until fragrant.

Create the Sauce:

1. Pour in fresh lemon juice, dry white wine (ensure it's gluten-free), and capers.
2. If you prefer a thicker sauce, dissolve 1 tablespoon of cornstarch (or gluten-free flour) in a small amount of water and add it to the sauce.

Simmer and Season:

1. Allow the sauce to simmer for about 5-7 minutes until it has reduced and thickened slightly.
2. Season with salt and freshly ground black pepper to taste. Adjust flavors as needed.

Gluten-Free Pasta Recommendations

To complete your Gluten-Free Chicken Piccata meal, you can serve it over gluten-free pasta. Here are some gluten-free pasta recommendations:

Brown Rice Pasta: Brown rice pasta is a versatile and gluten-free option that closely resembles traditional pasta in texture.

Quinoa Pasta: Quinoa pasta is protein-rich and has a slightly nutty flavor, making it a nutritious choice.

Chickpea Pasta: Chickpea pasta is high in protein and fiber, providing a heartier option for your dish.

Gluten-Free Corn Pasta: Corn pasta offers a mild, slightly sweet flavor and cooks similarly to wheat pasta.

Zucchini Noodles (Zoodles): For a low-carb and gluten-free alternative, consider using spiralized zucchini noodles.

Savoring Gluten-Free Delight

Gluten-Free Chicken Piccata offers a safe and delicious option for those with gluten sensitivities or dietary restrictions. With the right gluten-free ingredients, you can still enjoy the classic flavors of Chicken Piccata without compromise.

Chapter 16: Keto-Friendly Chicken Piccata

In this chapter, we're diving into a keto-friendly version of Chicken Piccata, designed for those following a low-carb ketogenic diet. Discover keto-friendly approaches, learn how to create a low-carb breading and coating for your chicken, prepare a keto lemon-caper sauce, and find keto side dishes and pairings to complete your keto meal.

Keto-Friendly Approaches

Enjoying a keto-friendly Chicken Piccata means reducing carbs while still savoring the flavors of this classic dish. We'll explore methods to create a keto-compliant version that fits within the low-carb parameters of a ketogenic diet.

Key Principles:

- Replace high-carb ingredients with low-carb alternatives.

- Focus on healthy fats and lean protein to stay in ketosis.

- Keep net carb count low while maximizing flavor.

Low-Carb Breading and Coating

Creating a low-carb breading and coating for your chicken is a crucial aspect of keto-friendly Chicken Piccata. Here are some low-carb options:

Almond Flour:

Almond flour is a versatile and keto-friendly choice for coating your chicken. It provides a nutty flavor and a satisfying crunch without the carbs.

Coconut Flour:

Coconut flour is another low-carb alternative that works well for breading chicken. It offers a subtle coconut flavor and helps create a crispy coating.

Pork Rinds:

Crushed pork rinds are a creative and keto-friendly option for breading. They provide a crunchy texture and a savory taste.

Parmesan Cheese:

Grated Parmesan cheese can serve as both a breading and a flavorful coating for your chicken. It's low in carbs and enhances the dish's taste.

Keto Lemon-Caper Sauce

To maintain the keto-friendliness of your Chicken Piccata, prepare a keto lemon-caper sauce. Here's how:

Ingredients for Keto Lemon-Caper Sauce:

- 2 tablespoons unsalted butter
- 1/4 cup fresh lemon juice (about 2 lemons)
- 1/4 cup dry white wine (or chicken broth)
- 2 tablespoons capers, drained and rinsed
- 1 clove garlic, minced
- Salt and freshly ground black pepper, to taste

Instructions:
Prepare the Keto Lemon-Caper Sauce:

1. In a small saucepan, melt unsalted butter over medium heat.

Create the Sauce:

1. Pour in fresh lemon juice, dry white wine (or chicken broth), capers, and minced garlic.

Simmer and Season:

1. Allow the sauce to simmer for about 5-7 minutes until it has reduced and thickened slightly.
2. Season with salt and freshly ground black pepper to taste. Adjust flavors as needed.

Keto Side Dishes and Pairings

To complete your keto-friendly Chicken Piccata meal, consider these keto side dishes and pairings:

Keto-Friendly Vegetable Medley: A combination of low-carb vegetables like broccoli, cauliflower, and asparagus, roasted in olive oil.

Cauliflower Rice: Serve your Chicken Piccata over cauliflower rice for a keto-friendly alternative to regular rice.

Keto Caesar Salad: A Caesar salad made with keto-friendly dressing, grated Parmesan cheese, and crisp romaine lettuce.

Zucchini Noodles (Zoodles): Replace traditional pasta with spiralized zucchini noodles for a low-carb option.

Avocado Salad: A simple salad featuring sliced avocado, cherry tomatoes, and a keto vinaigrette dressing.

Keto Delight with Flavor

Keto-Friendly Chicken Piccata allows you to indulge in this classic dish while adhering to your ketogenic lifestyle. By selecting low-carb alternatives and embracing healthy fats, you can enjoy the rich flavors without compromising your keto goals.

Chapter 17: Kid-Friendly Chicken Piccata

In this chapter, we're introducing a kid-friendly version of Chicken Piccata. We'll focus on creating a family-friendly Chicken Piccata that appeals to kids with milder flavor variations, the use of chicken tenders, and kid-friendly side dishes and accompaniments.

Family-Friendly Chicken Piccata

Chicken Piccata can be a delightful and family-friendly dish with a few adjustments. We'll ensure that the flavors are approachable for children while keeping the essence of this classic dish intact.

Key Considerations:

1. Mild flavor variations that kids are likely to enjoy.
2. Chicken tenders or boneless, skinless chicken thighs for kid-sized portions.
3. Kid-friendly side dishes and accompaniments.

Mild Flavor Variations

To cater to kids' tastes, consider these mild flavor variations for Chicken Piccata:

Reduced Lemon Zest: Use less lemon zest in the lemon-caper sauce to reduce the tanginess.

Less Garlic: Minimize the amount of garlic in the sauce for a milder flavor.

No Wine: Omit the dry white wine and use chicken broth for the sauce to eliminate alcohol content.

Chicken Tenders for Kids

Using chicken tenders or boneless, skinless chicken thighs is a great choice for kids. They are easier to handle, cook quickly, and are perfect for kid-sized portions.

Kid-Friendly Chicken Tenders Recipe:
Ingredients for Kid-Friendly Chicken Tenders:

- 1 pound chicken tenders
- Salt and pepper, to taste
- 1/2 cup all-purpose flour, for dredging
- 2 tablespoons olive oil

Instructions:

1. Season chicken tenders with salt and pepper.
2. Dredge each chicken tender in all-purpose flour, shaking off any excess.
3. Heat olive oil in a skillet over medium-high heat.
4. Cook the chicken tenders for about 3-4 minutes per side, or until they are golden brown and cooked through.

Kid-Friendly Sides and Accompaniments

Complete your Kid-Friendly Chicken Piccata meal with side dishes and accompaniments that children are likely to enjoy:

Mashed Potatoes: Creamy mashed potatoes are a comforting and familiar side dish for kids.

Buttered Noodles: Simple buttered noodles or pasta with a sprinkle of Parmesan cheese can be a hit with kids.

Steamed Green Beans: Steamed green beans with a touch of butter and a pinch of salt are a nutritious and kid-friendly option.

Sliced Carrots: Sliced and lightly steamed carrots are another vegetable option that kids often find appealing.

Applesauce: A small serving of unsweetened applesauce can complement the meal and provide a touch of sweetness.

Family Togetherness

Kid-Friendly Chicken Piccata is about bringing families together around the dinner table. By adjusting the flavors and using kid-sized portions, you can introduce your little ones to the joys of this classic dish and create cherished family moments.

Chapter 18: Piccata-Inspired Sides and Salads

In this chapter, we're exploring a variety of side dishes and salads that complement your Piccata dish beautifully. From fresh salads with Piccata flair to Piccata-inspired vegetable sides and bread and rolls to complete your meal, you'll find the perfect accompaniments to elevate your dining experience.

Complementing Your Piccata Dish

Enhancing your Piccata dish with thoughtfully chosen sides and salads can create a well-rounded and satisfying meal. These side dishes not only complement the flavors of Piccata but also add variety and freshness to your plate.

Fresh Salads with Piccata Flair

Lemon-Caper Salad

Ingredients:

- Mixed greens
- Cherry tomatoes, halved
- Cucumber slices
- Red onion slices
- Capers
- Lemon-caper vinaigrette (made with lemon juice, olive oil, capers, Dijon mustard, and honey)
- Freshly cracked black pepper

Instructions:

1. In a large salad bowl, combine mixed greens, cherry tomatoes, cucumber slices, and red onion slices.
2. Sprinkle capers over the salad.
3. Drizzle the lemon-caper vinaigrette over the salad.

4. Season with freshly cracked black pepper to taste.

Piccata Potato Salad
Ingredients:

- Potatoes, boiled and cubed
- Chopped fresh parsley
- Red onion, finely chopped
- Capers
- Lemon-caper dressing (made with lemon juice, olive oil, capers, Dijon mustard, and honey)
- Salt and freshly ground black pepper

Instructions:

1. In a large bowl, combine the boiled and cubed potatoes, chopped fresh parsley, finely chopped red onion, and capers.
2. Drizzle the lemon-caper dressing over the salad.
3. Season with salt and freshly ground black pepper to taste.

Piccata-Inspired Vegetable Sides
Garlic Butter Asparagus
Ingredients:

- Fresh asparagus spears
- Garlic butter sauce (melted butter with minced garlic)
- Lemon zest
- Grated Parmesan cheese
- Salt and freshly ground black pepper

Instructions:

1. Toss asparagus spears in the garlic butter sauce.

2. Sprinkle with lemon zest, grated Parmesan cheese, salt, and freshly ground black pepper.
3. Roast or grill until tender.

Lemon-Herb Roasted Potatoes
Ingredients:

- Small potatoes, halved
- Olive oil
- Fresh lemon juice
- Chopped fresh herbs (such as rosemary and thyme)
- Lemon zest
- Salt and freshly ground black pepper

Instructions:

1. Toss halved potatoes in olive oil, fresh lemon juice, chopped fresh herbs, and lemon zest.
2. Season with salt and freshly ground black pepper.
3. Roast until golden brown and tender.

Bread and Rolls
Garlic Bread
Ingredients:

- Baguette or Italian bread
- Unsalted butter, softened
- Minced garlic
- Chopped fresh parsley
- Grated Parmesan cheese

Instructions:

1. Slice the baguette or Italian bread in half lengthwise.
2. Mix minced garlic, chopped fresh parsley, and grated Parmesan cheese into softened unsalted butter.
3. Spread the garlic butter mixture on the cut sides of the bread.
4. Bake until the bread is toasted and the butter is melted and bubbling.

Elevate Your Dining Experience

With Piccata-inspired sides and salads, you can elevate your Piccata dish into a complete and delightful meal. Whether you're looking for freshness, crunch, or comforting warmth, these accompaniments are designed to enhance your dining experience.

Chapter 19: Perfect Pairings

In this chapter, we're exploring the art of perfect pairings to accompany your Chicken Piccata dish. Whether you're seeking non-alcoholic options or aiming to create a memorable dining experience, we have suggestions to enhance your meal.

Non-Alcoholic Options
Lemon and Herb Infused Water
Ingredients:

- Water
- Slices of fresh lemon
- Fresh herbs (such as rosemary and mint)

Instructions:

1. Fill a pitcher with water.
2. Add slices of fresh lemon and a few sprigs of fresh herbs.
3. Allow the flavors to infuse for at least 30 minutes before serving.

Sparkling Citrus Cooler
Ingredients:

- Sparkling water or club soda
- Freshly squeezed citrus juice (e.g., lemon, lime, or orange)
- A touch of honey or a sugar-free sweetener (optional)
- Slices of citrus for garnish
- Ice cubes

Instructions:

1. In a glass, combine sparkling water, freshly squeezed citrus juice, and sweetener if desired.
2. Add ice cubes and garnish with slices of citrus.

Creating a Memorable Dining Experience

To elevate your dining experience while serving Chicken Piccata, consider these tips:

Table Setting: Arrange a beautifully set table with elegant dinnerware, flatware, and glassware to create an inviting atmosphere.

Candlelight: Add the warm glow of candles to your dining area for a cozy and romantic ambiance, especially for evening meals.

Fresh Flowers: A vase of fresh flowers can brighten up your table and add a touch of nature to your dining space.

Music: Play soft background music that complements the mood you want to create, whether it's soothing jazz or classical melodies.

Personal Touch: Consider adding a handwritten menu or a special message for your guests to make the meal feel more personal.

Unforgettable Moments

Pairing your Chicken Piccata with the right non-alcoholic beverages and creating a memorable dining setting can turn a meal into an unforgettable moment. Whether you're dining with loved ones or indulging in a solo culinary adventure, these thoughtful touches can enhance the experience.

Chapter 20: Desserts with a Piccata Twist

In this chapter, we're exploring delightful desserts with a Piccata twist to provide sweet endings to your Piccata feast. From lemon desserts and treats to Piccata-flavored dessert creations, you'll discover a variety of ways to finish your meal on a sweet note.

Sweet Endings to Your Piccata Feast

After enjoying a savory and satisfying Chicken Piccata, it's time to indulge in desserts that complement the flavors and refresh your palate. These dessert ideas are inspired by the bright and zesty elements of Piccata dishes.

Lemon Desserts and Treats

Lemon Sorbet

Ingredients:

- Fresh lemon juice
- Lemon zest
- Sugar (or a sugar substitute for a lower-carb option)
- Water

Instructions:

1. Combine fresh lemon juice, lemon zest, sugar, and water in a saucepan.
2. Heat the mixture over medium heat until the sugar is dissolved.
3. Remove from heat and let it cool.
4. Churn the mixture in an ice cream maker according to the manufacturer's instructions.
5. Freeze until firm, then serve.

Lemon Bars

Ingredients:

- Butter
- Sugar (or a sugar substitute)
- Flour (or almond flour for a gluten-free option)
- Eggs
- Fresh lemon juice and zest
- Powdered sugar for dusting

Instructions:

1. Prepare a buttery shortbread crust and bake it until golden brown.
2. Mix eggs, sugar, fresh lemon juice, and zest to create the lemon filling.
3. Pour the lemon filling over the baked crust and return to the oven until set.
4. Let it cool, dust with powdered sugar, and cut into bars.

Piccata-Flavored Dessert Creations
Lemon-Caper Cookies
Ingredients:

- Butter
- Sugar (or a sugar substitute)
- Flour (or almond flour for a gluten-free option)
- Lemon zest
- Capers, finely chopped
- Powdered sugar for dusting

Instructions:

1. Cream butter and sugar together.

2. Mix in flour, lemon zest, and finely chopped capers.
3. Shape the dough into cookies and bake until lightly golden.
4. Dust with powdered sugar before serving.

Lemon-Caper Pound Cake
Ingredients:

- Butter
- Sugar (or a sugar substitute)
- Flour (or almond flour for a gluten-free option)
- Eggs
- Lemon juice and zest
- Capers, finely chopped
- Baking powder
- Salt

Instructions:

1. Cream butter and sugar together.
2. Mix in eggs, lemon juice, and zest.
3. Fold in flour, finely chopped capers, baking powder, and salt.
4. Bake in a loaf pan until a toothpick comes out clean.
5. Let it cool, then slice and serve.

Finishing Your Meal on a Sweet Note

Desserts with a Piccata twist bring a delightful and refreshing conclusion to your meal. Whether you opt for a zesty lemon sorbet, classic lemon bars, or inventive lemon-caper treats, you're sure to satisfy your sweet tooth with a touch of Piccata flair.

Milton Keynes UK
Ingram Content Group UK Ltd.
UKHW010616291123
433416UK00001B/113